IS MANKIND INTELLIGENT YET?

IS MANKIND INTELLIGENT YET?

C. G. Sayer

Book Guild Publishing
Sussex, England

First published in Great Britain in 2010 by
The Book Guild Ltd
Pavilion View
19 New Road
Brighton, BN1 1UF

Typesetting in Garamond by
SetSystems Ltd, Saffron Walden, Essex

Printed in Great Britain by
CPI Antony Rowe

A catalogue record for this book is available from
the British Library

ISBN 978 1 84624 490 2

Said by a clever eight-and-a-half year old on 14 January 2002:

'Man is clever because he has invented weapons.'
I wonder if an eight-and-a-half year old child in 3002
will be able to say, 'I know mankind is intelligent
because we threw away our weapons.'?

Contents

CONTENTS

Foreword

These thoughts are considering Mankind as a species.

Individuals and groups can and do achieve great things with dedication and forethought . . . but it is Mankind as a species that inhabits our planet.

Is Mankind, as a species, deeply flawed, or does it have the potential to develop into a truly intelligent species – a success in evolutionary terms?

A further theme is the extent to which Mankind can, with any justification, claim to be different from, separate from or superior to the other creatures with which we share the planet.

This is largely a book of questions from a complete layman, who is asking them not because he thinks he knows the answers, but because he knows that he does not.

Only two statements seem to the author to be self-evident truth – 'Violence is failure' and 'Mankind is not yet intelligent'.

C. G. Sayer, 2010

Acknowledgements

I would like to thank Mr Peter Buekers for the interest he has shown in this project which kick-started me back into action and made me believe it might eventually come to fruition, for his thought-provoking comments and for 'incipiens'.

However, above all my thanks go to my long-suffering and very patient wife, with whom I have discussed the entire contents of this book. Without her regular and active encouragement you would not be reading this now: there would be no book at all.

Introduction

A question

Suppose that you are on a voyage through the universe, searching out all planets that have life-forms on them. Would you expect to find that the most advanced species on every inhabited planet has two features that distinguish it from all the other life-forms on the planet:

1. it routinely and regularly kills large numbers of its own species, and
2. it degrades the planet it lives on?

. . . and some conclusions

If the answer is 'Yes', then the outcome of evolution in the universe to date seems quite extraordinary – at its very pinnacle is always a self-destructive species.

If the answer is 'No', then surely we must consider the proposition that Man is a seriously flawed branch of evolution?

If your answer is that there is no other life in the universe apart from that on earth, then the most advanced species in existence regularly kills large numbers of its own species, unlike all other life-forms in the universe, and degrades the only inhabited planet.

Whichever is your answer, the situation upon earth needs to be considered very thoroughly now, and especially now. Humans stand in some perplexity on an entirely new threshold – not that of a new millennium, but of knowledge of an entirely different order from that which we have acquired hitherto. This new knowledge raises absolutely fundamental questions.

These questions involve considering ourselves, our existence on earth, our relationship with the earth and all its inhabitants and even, eventually, our situation in the universe.

Awe Inspiring

How did an advanced species occur on earth?

Take some hydrogen and some helium, mix thoroughly and then sit back and listen to Mozart while looking at a Rembrandt portrait . . . having allowed some 13 billion years to elapse between mixing and sitting down.

Can there be a more awe-inspiring concept than that a massive instantaneous event can occur in an empty void, which generates enough material, almost exclusively in the form of hydrogen and helium, eventually to create everything in our vast universe?

In the intervening years the original gases and their by-products have combined and recombined to become stars which have grown and died, creating new generations of stars and thus the entire range of substances in the universe.

Each of us can look at the night sky and see light that is millions of years old, reaching us from billions of miles away. We can look inside our bodies and see structures that originated on earth billions of years ago and have developed to make our own existence possible.

Which is a more magnificent scenario – that we humans are an 'extra' on a single planet, alone in an otherwise empty, huge universe, or that we are an evolving part of this massive

3

continuum stretching onwards from the original helium/hydrogen event? Not alone, but part of a wonderful universe, with ancestry stretching back billions of years.

Is an acorn alive? If you hold an acorn in your hand it seems incredible that it may one day weigh many tons and live some 800 years, if conditions are right for the life dormant within it to flourish. The acorn can do this because the potential for life was put there by the tree. So, is the acorn itself alive?

Is the universe alive?

The Big Bang may well have generated a universe which itself creates life from non-life, this life then flourishing wherever and whenever it is remotely possible. This seems to be the case on earth – life in the sea, on the land, in complete darkness at fumaroles at the bottom of the sea, in volcanic pools, in the human gut, and so on. And if on earth, why not throughout the universe?

A life-creating universe. Simple words but, if true, surely a sublime concept? A universe that created itself, once the simple building blocks appeared, and that itself creates life as if life was built into the Big Bang itself. Is it possible that the Big Bang was like the acorn with life-creation built into it? Could any concept be more awe inspiring?

This all ignores the notion that the Big Bang appeared in the void from Nowhere, or as if from Nowhere. So does life-creation appear to originate in Nowhere, as the life within the acorn originates in the tree?

Might there be a regression of Nowheres, stretching back into infinity, or to some prime creating force?

Intelligence?

Is Mankind intelligent? Clever, certainly. But intelligent? Surely not? Surely cleverness is involved in making and discovering things, while intelligence must also be concerned with what you *do* with what you make and discover?

Who says that Mankind is intelligent? Mankind, who devised the concept and has been consistently failing to achieve it.

I have taken various examinations. I have never devised the syllabus, set the examination paper, taken the exam, marked my paper myself, *failed* the examination and given myself a pass mark.

Mankind has decided that it is intelligent. A definition of intelligence is the faculty of knowing, understanding and reasoning. Surely the outcome of this faculty should be the ability both to tackle problems and to consider the results of what one is doing? If one can know, understand and reason but be unable (or is it unwilling?) to solve problems or to evaluate one's solutions, then one's 'intelligence' must surely be extremely suspect.

So is intelligence the ability to solve easy problems?

We have discovered how to map the universe, investigate the atom, go to the moon, devise the internal combustion engine, build skyscrapers and computers and start understanding the genome. All of these are notable achievements. All are knowledge standing on the shoulders of previous discoveries. Many of our achievements do solve problems, while not a few create worse ones.

But are these the difficult problems? Are they even the important ones?

Which, for example, is more significant? Getting to the moon about 40 years ago or eradicating poliomyelitis from our whole planet, rather than from only the affluent areas? This is only now being attempted by charitable effort. Can the members of Mankind live together in peace? Does Mankind know how to ensure that none of its members lives in poverty or misery? Can Mankind live on this planet without degrading it?

Are these difficult problems actually insoluble? Or is Mankind's assessment of intelligence only 'an ability to solve simple problems'?

Has Mankind set the bar at the level 'Being unable to solve difficult problems', jumped over the bar and announced, 'We are intelligent'? Rather as if a hurdler was proud of being able to run extremely fast, while being unable to jump hurdles.

We have called some of our ancestors *Homo habilis* (we might say 'clever man') and ourselves *Homo sapiens* (we might say 'intelligent man'). Are we really *Homo sapiens* yet?

In a nutshell, can a species describe itself as intelligent if it has got to the moon and not eradicated polio? Can it even evaluate the relative significance of problems, never mind solve them?

Does Mankind perhaps need a new concept beyond mere intelligence, a word such as *ultelligence*, being intelligence that:

1. evaluates the significance of problems,
2. focuses on the most pressing and

3. considers comprehensively the outcomes of any
   contemplated actions?

If the cleverest species on a planet is not at the same time truly
intelligent, there is a disastrous situation for all life on the
planet. Mankind will presumably eventually have the capability
to render the planet sterile and lifeless, whether by accident or
design. Can we be sure that we shall not, considering our past
performance?

One might use other definitions, such as that intelligence is
the capacity and desire to learn beyond one's basic instincts, but
surely every definition needs to include evaluating the outcome
of what one does? Can a clever action which has an unfortunate
and avoidable result ever be regarded as an intelligent action?

Mankind in Perspective

We inhabit this planet along with millions of other creatures. Not only are we the masters of our own planet, but we have just started voyaging out into the universe. We have already sent out probes announcing our presence. We are well aware of our significant and positive role in the scheme of things.

However, although we are aware of this, I am not in the least convinced that the other creatures on our planet, if they could be asked, would agree. If you could ask an antelope, a frog or an eagle to name the most significant creature on earth exerting a positive influence on the overall balance of life, I do not suppose that Man would figure anywhere on the list at all. Why should we? The dung-beetle, the bacteria that break down detritus into soil, the worm, the bee – creatures like these would all have serious claims. Surely Man is only positively significant to himself (and dogs)?

If the choice were for the most significant creature on earth exerting a *negative* influence on the balance of life, then presumably Man would be fighting it out with those such as the mosquito and the tapeworm, in the view of all the others on earth. Probably this is unfair to the mosquito and tapeworm as they are not so much randomly and thoroughly destructive, as creatures with niches in a balanced whole.

9

'Bestial' is a word created by humans and it means 'behaving like a (degenerate) human'. Animals do not indulge in 'bestial' behaviour. Surely this word tells us a great deal about humans and absolutely nothing about animals? In using this word, is Mankind struggling to describe an entirely false superiority?

Once an animal or group of animals, not intelligent, has established a territory that can sustain it, there does not seem to be much of an urge to go and 'capture' another territory. A pride of lions, most ferocious beasts, would presumably regard it as a ridiculous suggestion that it should go and attack another whole pride of lions in order to 'control' extra territory which it did not need. I would suppose that the lions' most likely response would be to ask, 'Why?'

Clearly many creatures require a territory to survive in, and may defend it if need be, but do many creatures attempt to acquire territory that they do not need? Indeed, do many creatures indulge in war at all?

Man, however, measures his 'intelligence' as vastly superior to the lion, and marches off many miles to fight an enemy who later on will march many miles back to do the same. He has been doing this regularly since the time of Eannatum, King of Lagash, in the Middle East and presumably well before that. It seems that Eannatum conquered Umma in 2900 BC. One hundred years later, apparently, Lagai-Zaggisi, ruler of Umma, destroyed Lagash. And we are still at it today, as I write.

It seems that some monkeys, though not all, do display belligerence, apparently for the sake of it, just as we do. Perhaps we would therefore claim this shows that they, too, are 'intelligent'?

We must not forget that it is Man who has defined the 'intelligence' that he measures and which renders him superior. We cannot measure 'humanity', 'compassion', 'creativity', 'ability to

live within our environment', 'ability to cooperate', 'far sighted-
ness' – and as we cannot, we do not include these in our overall
measurement of 'IQ'. So we measure 'intelligence' and, though
we are not at all sure what it is that we have measured, we base
our superiority over our fellow creatures mainly on this one
elusive feature, which certainly excludes the ability to live in
harmony with ourselves or our planet.

I am merely a child of my times. I happen to think that sea
levels may well rise some 20 or more feet over the next 300 to
400 years as almost all the ice on earth melts. THIS IS AN
ENTIRELY UNSCIENTIFIC PERSONAL GUESS, but that
is irrelevant. It is what I think – AND I DO NOT CARE
ABOUT ANY POSSIBLE DISASTROUS RESULTS. If I am
right, many islands would vanish, many low-lying areas, such as
much of Florida, Holland, Bangladesh, Northern Europe, England, and so on, would be flooded to a greater or lesser degree
Every harbour in the world would be submerged. Farming land
and living space would be lost across the world. Rivers that rely
on glaciers would never be the same agasin.

To believe that we, today, may be causing or exacerbating
such future disasters, *and not to care about it* cannot, in my
view, be regarded as intelligent behaviour. I am indeed a child
of my time.

Social Behaviour

We do not include 'the ability to assess the effects of our actions on others' in our concept of intelligence. Yet surely it is one of the most important aspects of true intelligence on a personal and on a global scale? Anyone who does not or cannot evaluate the effect of his/her actions on the feelings and lives of others is at best a nuisance and at worst a disaster. And is surely a malfunctioning human, unless you regard this ability as of no fundamental significance. This applies to an even greater degree on a national and global scale. If the effects of my actions and choices on the lives of other humans across the planet are of no significance for me, what right have I to claim to be 'intelligent' at all?

'Intelligence' in an individual, as measured by humans today, certainly does not mean that the individual cannot also be extremely stupid. A highly 'intelligent' person may be hopeless at personal relationships and at managing daily life, and may be thoroughly blinkered and uncooperative. How can humans describe one of their kind as 'intelligent' when (s)he blunders about life causing chaos? Or how can Mankind have the gall to describe itself as an intelligent life-form when it has so far been blundering through history causing chaos at every level from the personal to the global?

It is suggested that intelligence means the ability to solve problems – but not the problems of life, personal or global. It might seem not only reasonable, but also obvious, to suggest that an individual can be both intelligent and deficient in the literal sense of being deficient as a human. Hitler could not possibly have achieved all the damage that he did, if he had not had a considerable amount of what we call intelligence. Can we just leave it at that? A man can be a human catastrophe and our best description is that he was intelligent but evil.

What is the value in a word, 'intelligence', that can both be used to distinguish us from the animal kingdom and be applied to Idi Amin, Hitler, Pol Pot, and the like?

Evil

Surely the concept of 'evil' is a cop-out?

Suppose one suggested that to be a full member of an advanced intelligent species is to live well with and for the other members of one's species, in harmony with one's environment . . . and that anything less is to be less than a fully functioning member of that species. Is that a ridiculous suggestion?

If it is ridiculous, then no advanced species in the universe can be expected to live in harmony as a species, or with its environment. An unduly pessimistic prospect?

If it is not a ridiculous suggestion, then could Mankind live like this? After all, most humans do appear to wish to live in harmony. What percentage of humans wish to be antisocial themselves or to be surrounded by antisocial behaviour?

Is it then possible that humans have indeed evolved to be fundamentally positive and cooperative within their species, like

14

termites, bees and zebras to name a few? Indeed, is it then a possibility that a *true* human is fundamentally positive, cooperative and non-violent, wishing to live in such a society? If so, why is there violence, war and pollution?

'Evil' is a handy explanation. Either it is an extraneous invader, like measles or smallpox, which individuals should resist, or it is basic to humankind at birth, or both.

We have developed 'intelligence' so we have been able to propose 'evil' to explain our shortcomings. So we can say that a serial killer is evil. Just as witches were evil? Or those with schizophrenia were possessed by the devil? Are we now wrong to suggest that they are suffering from a medical condition?

Of course, maybe now, in the twenty-first century, we do know all the answers, unlike those living in the Middle Ages, who only thought they knew. Or do we understand criminality, violence and antisocial behaviour about as well as they understood schizophrenia in the Middle Ages?

Suppose a serial killer is obviously ill, just by being a serial killer. As obviously ill as someone with smallpox. Could this apply, in varying degrees, to anyone who commits murder or uses violence? Or commits any antisocial acts?

Will they look back in AD 3000 with amazement at us, the people of the twenty-first century, and marvel that we were still using 'evil' as a smokescreen for our own ignorance of the causes of wrongdoing?

If someone is ill, the idea is to cure them. If we regarded being ill as requiring punishment instead of treatment, recidivism among patients would surely be rather high.

Society does not even blame someone for being ill if they have chosen to become ill, say by smoking or drinking. A person with lung cancer now almost certainly chose to get it by smoking, by exercising free will, and yet (s)he is still regarded as ill and in need of medical help. Hospitals try to save people who have destroyed their health by drinking.

It is a self-evident truth that Mankind aims to cure illness.

Criminality

The greatest and most far-reaching improvements in health came from discoveries such as that cholera came from drinking contaminated water, from the introduction of proper sewage systems and the invention of vaccination. Practices like these revolutionised health care. But these measures struck at the roots of illness: they did not fix the problem *after* people fell ill – they stopped people from falling ill in the first place.

Surely in almost every case criminality and antisocial behaviour are acquired, just as many diseases are?

So, stopping people from starting on criminality and antisocial behaviour will be as significant an approach to these problems as introducing clean water, sewage treatment and vaccination were to the problems of ill-health. This might be cheaper than being 'tough on crime' in the medium to long term. And, unlike today's medical care, the likely costs would presumably not increase with the individual's age.

Even if this approach were more expensive than our present anti-crime efforts, would it not be worth the money to reduce or even eliminate the suffering of victims and the damage done by and to the perpetrators?

The problem is that people had to understand how and why cholera and other diseases arose and spread before they could eliminate them.

Saying 'prison works' is like saying that doctors can cure

many of the people with cholera, none of whom should have had cholera in the first place.

Punishing criminality is straightforward. A term in prison; 'pay your dues'; a high percentage of recidivism; another term in prison; and so on. Straightforward. And very little requirement for the individual to face up to the hurt or damage caused by his/her actions.

Is having more and more people in prison really a measure of success? Is it really a success if around one per cent of a nation's adult population is in prison, as is now the case apparently in one highly developed country (ten times as many per head of the population as in other developed countries)? Or are high numbers in prison a straightforward measure of national failure?

Let us suppose that Mankind comes to regard criminality as an illness and introduces widespread measures to prevent it being caught, as with cholera. Aberrant behaviour could, for example, be caused by a failure of binocular vision, which apparently may affect 500,000 children in England. This is a condition easily cured but not often diagnosed (because it costs money to diagnose), which can cause illiteracy, severe underachievement, low self-esteem and all that can follow from that. It is even now being suggested that some antisocial behaviour is linked to a hormone problem and that this condition occurs particularly in teenage years.

One new situation might be that parents who now call on the doctor if their child has a high temperature or pain would regard it as equally normal to seek medical help if their child were getting out of control or becoming aggressive. A child nowadays does not question being called 'ill' – this could presumably equally well apply if social failure were perceived as an illness like measles.

Then, when pupils first arrive in school or nursery school

their 'social health' could be assessed very rapidly as a matter of routine and appropriate action could be taken as a matter of course, just as if they were found to be suffering from tuberculosis. The action would presumably not just involve the individual child but all contributing factors. (However, I am certainly, not suggesting that the appropriate response would be pills or potions!)

In 2008, a report claimed that around 4000 children a year, aged from 2 to 5, are excluded from nursery schools in Britain for violent behaviour. For the age range 2 to 11 the figure was given as 45,000 a year. Surely this, though regrettable, is a golden opportunity? The system already has a 'sieve' available which identifies young children with social problems. These children are not wicked, evil or criminal, although they may grow into criminals. Why could they not be regarded as ill, which has no stigma attached, and be treated in exactly the same non-judgemental way as patients are treated today?

Clearly there would be problems: first, establishing what level of behaviour is actually not healthy; then, establishing what causes antisocial behaviour and criminality and what measures effectively reduce or even eradicate such attitudes early in life; then, deciding what kind of hospitals, including secure hospitals, are required for those adults who have succumbed; then, if criminality is to be cured once someone has succumbed to it, how do you cure it – and even more difficult, perhaps, how do you know when it is cured? And what do you do if you decide that someone cannot be cured?

But underlying these various problems would be another. No adult who is ill can normally be treated at all unless (s)he accepts being ill, alcoholism being an extreme example. Presumably it would likewise be impossible to cure any wrongdoer unless (s)he accepted the wrongness of the behaviour. Our present punitive system does not normally require any such acceptance. Much easier!

Retribution

'It is only human to seek revenge.'

Precisely. Only humans seek revenge It is a distinguishing feature of the human species. Is the urge for revenge a distinguishing feature of which Mankind can be proud? 'Revenge is only natural.' Well, yes. It is only 'natural' to humans.

Lethal family feuds have been known to carry on for generations. International politics in some parts of the world are clearly based on revenge. Wars very often result from previous wars.

States kill with premeditation, which would be called murder if the euphemistic word 'execution' had not been created in the process of giving such killing legal justification. Some of these states are Christian or otherwise religious, and so one might suppose that they believe in forgiveness and even repentance and restitution.

In considering whether an advanced species can claim to be intelligent, we may consider whether the species believes that violence can be, quite literally, legitimised in the form of revenge.

Was it intelligent to drown or burn witches and burn heretics? These activities were certainly legitimised when Mankind was perpetrating them. Maybe some of those reading this think we should still be doing this. After all, if those actions were intelligent then, why should they not be intelligent actions now?

If you find the drowning of witches and the burning of heretics at all unsatisfactory, why would you classify as satisfactory electrocuting, poisoning, hanging and shooting, which are our modern versions of drowning and burning transgressors? Some of these activities are not even necessarily quicker than the earlier ones.

Is it not strange that it is perfectly legal and acceptable to sell products which will most certainly kill some of those who use them entirely properly? This behaviour has been legitimised over centuries and to ban it would presumably be counterproductive, rendering cigarettes illegal and so more desirable. Of course you choose to smoke, almost invariably in your teens, and you choose not to give up, so you may kill yourself. But is it not still strange that you can legitimately provide a lethal product, in a perfectly premeditated fashion, but if you kill someone in an unpremeditated manner you may not only be punished by imprisonment but also be poisoned, hanged or electrocuted by the state?

Will they look back from AD 3000 and see the killing of prisoners in the twenty-first century as just as intelligent as the killing of witches and heretics in the Middle Ages? And will revenge still be regarded as 'natural'?

Language

There seems to be a notion that Mankind is set apart from the rest of creation by the use of language. Surely this is a complete fallacy? Would it not be completely incredible if an advanced species did not have language? Language is built into the structure of the world. Language is all around us on earth.

To suggest that language could not have existed before Man arrived to codify it seems entirely arrogant. If a slug could not *go left, right* or *forwards* it would soon be a dead slug. Likewise if it could not go *up* a *stalk* or perceive a *leaf* or *eat* it. It has no knowledge of words or language – but it is 'living language'.

Surely, what Man has done is to perceive the 'language of life', put words to it, and then develop Mankind's language into a reasonably efficient communication system, and has since been claiming to have invented language? This is much like a chicken that has laid an egg and then starts crowing about having invented reproduction.

Our human level of language is quite impressive but still allows misinterpretation and is sorely inadequate in some areas, such as conveying visual images or complex emotional states.

Language is the 'parts of speech' and their use. All around us are to be seen nouns (trees, sky), verbs (fall, grow), adjectives

21

(red, blue), adverbs (suddenly, slowly), prepositions (up, around), and so on, even including conjunctions (if, and).

What Man has done is to give all these things names, both the concepts themselves and the grammatical terms for the concepts, and has then gone on to be able to consider and discuss abstract thoughts and ideas. What Man has most certainly NOT done, is to create the trees, rain falling, the colours, or any other part of the language of life that surrounds us.

Nor has Man, either in spoken or in written language, invented communication. A bee that finds food returns to the hive and communicates to the others where to find it, by 'dancing'. Man, because he is 'intelligent', can point out that the bee is not using language when it is explaining direction and distance (both noun concepts) and the other bees are understanding it, but only 'delivering a message'.

If the bee was saying *The food source is about 200 yards southwest of the hive*, then that would be language. However, the bee is merely dancing about while the other bees are understanding that *the food source is about 200 yards southwest of the hive* – and off they go.

Ants go foraging and if one ant finds a food source then in a very short time the food is likely to be covered in ants. Clearly the forager has indicated where to find it. Again the information exchanged involves direction and target information, presumably given by the ant laying a trail back from the food to the nest. If the ant finds no food, it lays no trail, or at least not one that says 'Food this way'.

At the other end of the scale whales, elephants and dolphins clearly communicate, maybe at much higher levels than many other creatures, and we are now striving to understand this. So Mankind kills elephants for ivory trinkets, whales for no purpose at all and dolphins by accident, thus demonstrating our superiority as a species.

Indeed, was not the 'language of life' there before there was any life at all? When the earth began the 'rocks' were 'hard' or 'molten'. The volcanoes 'cast' their vapours 'upwards'. When uni-cellular life was starting up in the seas, it would 'float' or 'swim', 'consume' its 'food', 'divide' or 'conjugate'. All this was happening very satisfactorily before humans invented their grammatical terms to classify these activities.

Surely the language of life, which Mankind has codified into written and spoken forms, was all around on earth five billion years before we arrived?

Later, also, it would be extraordinary if the individuals in the herds of dinosaurs did not communicate with each other. A penguin mother can find the cry of its young among many hundreds or thousands of other baby penguins. If I walk near a blackbird's nest in our garden, its warning cry of danger is obvious. Blackbirds were presumably doing this long before humans arrived and other blackbirds were understanding the cry. Newly fledged baby birds call vociferously to their parents in their early flying days – and the parents call back. It is claimed that meerkats give warnings of specific dangers, such as a bird raptor or an animal hunter.

Surely communication existed long before humans were even a twinkle in a mammal's eye in the Cretaceous era?

Could advanced life on another planet similar to ours have a language which did not express noun, verb and preposition concepts? Putting it another way, would not a super-amoeba, if it developed language, have to use exactly the same grammar concepts as we do, with only the words differing? So surely all our grammar is dictated to us entirely by our surroundings.

Indeed, is it fanciful to suggest that the language on which we pride ourselves is actually built into the structure of the universe? All of our grammar is out there in space in the stars 'shining' and 'exploding', 'small' planets and 'huge' stars, all flying 'away' from each other. All of our grammar is happening out there every day.

Or rather, more than our grammar, more than our language. Some fish on earth, and some birds it seems, can detect, measure and use the earth's magnetic field to tell them which way they should be going. We have no such ability.

If we could, like these birds and fish, sense the earth's magnetic field, then quite possibly this would introduce quite new, different and unimaginable concepts into our grammar and language. So our human language is not merely only fairly accurate, but also incomplete.

If this were so, then Mankind's language ability is only an incomplete reflection of the language of life. Surely we have not invented language, merely discovered parts of it?

Thought

Surely much of thought does not need language?

Jasper, a dog of ours, had free access to the common behind our house and sometimes met another dog there. Then the other dog grew old and no longer went on the common.

One day Jasper went to the house where the other dog lived and knocked on the door, though how he did this the neighbours did not know. The Lady of the House opened the door. She had never seen Jasper before, but her son told her that this was the dog that their dog ran with on the common. So Jasper was allowed in. He went into the sitting room, lay down on the rug beside his friend for about twenty minutes, then got up and asked to be let out. He did this regularly for some years.

Then the other dog died. Jasper came as usual, and found his friend was not there. He only came once more; his friend was again not there, so he stopped coming. We had no idea that this had been happening until after Jasper also died.

No human was involved in Jasper going to the house or in his knocking on the door. These were the dog's own decisions. Likewise, no human was involved in his only going twice after the other dog had died. Again, his decision.

Surely these three decisions can hardly be instinct? If, however, they are to be classified as just instinct then what price any or all of our human decisions? Do we, like dogs, only function by instinct (but call our decisions thought)?

If we allow these decisions to be genuine thought, then presumably they were made without the conscious use of language. Or can it be that dogs internalise language? We humans might say, 'I shall visit my friend.' Surely it is inconceivable that a dog can visit the house of another dog without being aware of:

1. its own existence and
2. the existence of the dog it wishes to visit – i.e. 'I' and 'friend'.

This decision will have been taken each time at home, in the garden or on the common, so surely Jasper knew that he was *going*, and going to *visit* (not to stay for ever). So surely he knew, before he set off '*I* am *going* to *visit* my *friend*'?

And the difference between Jasper and us in such a situation? Is it not merely that we have given names, both *abstract* (pronoun, verb, noun) and *specific* (I, visit, friend) to the same thoughts that Jasper had? Surely our human achievement in this respect is the naming of parts – and not the use of thought itself?

One morning I was standing in a newly delivered office building, wondering where to route the electrical wiring. I thought about drilling horizontal holes through the vertical timbers to run the wire through the wall space before adding insulation and cladding. I also thought of running it up into the roof space and down again. And I thought of putting it into plastic channelling fixed to the surface of the wall cladding. All good human rationalising.

I was just favouring fitting it into the wall space before

putting the wall cladding on, when I realised that I was looking at the floor and the base of the wall, and seeing the wire running along the floor, below the bottom of the wall surface which did not need to reach right to the floor. I then saw a simple skirting board covering the wire. Much the best solution – but this was 'visualised' thinking, without any words being involved as far as I could tell.

About half an hour later we were sitting in the garden when a tiny shrew came scuttling across the lawn. Finally, two feet away from where we were sitting, it noticed us and froze. Instinct, just as I jump at a sudden unexpected noise. However, when I moved it ran straight to a small cleft in the base of the pear tree and vanished. I knew where it was, but it had disappeared behind a small tuft of grass just in front of the cleft in the trunk.

In what way were we different, the shrew and I? Each of us saw the solution to our problem. I most certainly did not see the solution because I knew the words 'wire', 'wall', 'floor', 'cladding' (in fact I suspect 'cladding' may be the wrong word), 'below', or 'put'. Indeed, how much of our daily thought *ever* involves the use of words: do the words come afterwards?

Surely neither the shrew nor I could manage to live one day satisfactorily if we could not think effectively?

Surely, then, I am merely part of an evolutionary continuum from a shrew-like creature running between the legs of the dinosaurs? That creature could think and so can I. Surely also, in the twenty-first century am I not part of an existing continuum which includes the shrew and me today?

We certainly, as a species, have more developed abilities than the shrew, but the significant thing is not that we have these abilities, but what we do with them as individuals and as a species.

Feeling

Love and compassion are clearly concepts of a very high order and Mankind rightly values them. Have we any right to regard these qualities as unique to us? If so, do we classify similar behaviour that appears to occur in other species as just 'instinct'? If so, let us beware!

Surely the use of 'instinct' in this context may be at best a smokescreen and at worst an own-goal, leading to the idea that Mankind's own behaviours may also be instinct?

Higher animal species, such as elephants, have been observed being clearly at least disconcerted, if not actually upset, by the death of one of them.

Our dog, Jasper, who figured in the previous chapter, was quite clearly sorely troubled by the death of his mother after they had lived with us together for a number of years. Indeed, it seemed very likely that he himself would not last very long after her death – until we acquired a new puppy. He was then transformed and restored to his previous lively self.

Innumerable thousands of species on this planet care for their young for varying lengths of time after they are born. The very fact there are also thousands of species that do not have any contact with their offspring after producing them makes the behaviour of those that do the more noteworthy.

'Well, of course, the continuation of one's species is fundamental to the whole concept of life. No continuation = no Life.'

So it is perfectly reasonable to say that the drive to continue the procreation of one's species is a matter of instinct. But there is a whole ladder of varying commitment to the nurturing of the young produced, from no commitment at all through days, weeks, months and years of such commitment.

The amount of effort involved in birds' care of their chicks is considerable and may, for example, eventually involve green woodpecker adults vociferously encouraging their chicks to make their first flight and then showing them where and how to find food. Or a spotted woodpecker persevering in convincing its chick that pecking the actual peanuts in a peanut holder is more productive than pecking the wooden back of the holder!

If even earwigs care for their young, and elephants spend months doing so, then surely our species' concern for our children is part of the natural continuum, even though it lasts much longer?

Surely Man is hardly more separate from the rest of life on this planet in respect of caring for others than is a chicken or an earwig?

Self-awareness

I know that I exist, on earth, in a solar system, in the universe.

Mind you, it might be truer to say that I believe I know about the earth, the solar system and the universe, as I have to take all this information on trust from others. However, I do know that I exist. Self-awareness is said to be another of the distinguishing features of the human.

We have had two dogs living with us at the same time. If self-awareness is a distinguishing feature of the human, then each of the two dogs was not aware of its own existence. If you have two dogs, it might not be clever to put their food randomly into one of two identical bowls each day, as this might well lead to quarrels. Certainly we always put the food for each dog into one specific bowl each day. Each dog would then go to its own bowl. Indeed, when one of them took to picking up a bowl and dropping it very audibly on the floor when he felt he wanted a biscuit, he always picked up his own.

Now neither dog, presumably, had language as we know it, but is it simply fanciful to observe that each dog knew perfectly well which bowl was 'mine' and which 'not mine' ('yours')? If a dog knows that 'this bowl is mine', how can it possibly not be self-aware?

Some birds mate for life and some always nest in the same

place, some after flying thousands of miles to get there. These birds can distinguish 'my' mate and 'my' nesting place. It is easy for us to say that this is merely instinct acting through the genes, but if a bird has no self-awareness, how can it sustain its awareness of 'my' mate and 'my' nesting place over time? Surely this is a logical impossibility?

Maybe we should be careful about designating the rest of life on earth as 'other than us'. Maybe the only justification is our own need to believe in our own significance.

And maybe, too, we should beware. If we are actually right and all the rest of life on earth is really unaware of its own existence, perhaps we too are kidding ourselves. Maybe our own 'self-awareness' is merely an aspect/expression of instinct, obfuscated by our ability to use language to confuse ourselves.

Because I can talk about the universe does not remotely mean that I really understand what I am talking about.

If earth received a truly advanced visitor from outer space, might it/(s)he indeed hear us discussing our 'self-awareness' and smile condescendingly. Such a visitor might be self-aware to a degree that we cannot even imagine. We are as aware of ourselves as clearly as our two dogs were, but do we 'know' ourselves much more than they did? We can recognise ourselves in a mirror (as can elephants and dolphins). Big deal. Does this mean that we are fully aware of ourselves – or aware of what a mirror is and how it works?

Are there degrees of self-awareness, with us perhaps only halfway along the scale?

Man's unique position . . . a new threshold

Billions of years ago photosynthetic bacteria created oxygen as a by-product of living their lives. They utterly transformed the earth. By creating oxygen they enabled the whole marvellous development of today's myriad life-forms to occur.

But, of course, they had no idea that they were doing this.

Mankind is on the threshold of being in the same position, of being able to transform the earth and life upon it.

But, unlike our far-distant precursors, we shall think we know what we are doing. An awesome responsibility. Never before has a species been in a position to transform the earth, while imagining that it knew what it was doing.

There are two ways in which we can and will exercise the responsibility of standing at this new threshold. The first is by the way we manage our daily lives. The second is an entirely new field of knowledge – our rudimentary understanding of the genome.

Just as the daily lives of those early organisms created what was, for them, a mere by-product, in the form of oxygen, so our daily lives are creating a whole range of by-products, but in our case many are poisons and problems, ranging from carbon dioxide to DDT, CFCs, mercury, radioactive waste, methane-producing waste dumps and so on and on. We also destroy forests which are probably very significant, we are changing the chemical composition of the seas, we are probably changing the earth's climate and we create ever huger cities. We have already started extinguishing species and regularly cause problems by the relocation of species which turn out to be harmful in their new environments. Our world population is growing apace and our appetite for ever more possessions, facilities and energy is voracious. Many of us are devoted to conspicuous consumption.

We tell ourselves that we know what we are doing and are 'managing these problems'. Or that there are no problems at all. We noticed the unfortunate effects of DDT and CFCs before the effects were too disastrous and seem to have acted in time to reduce their impact gradually.

Surely, however, in the field of damaging our earth, of fouling our nest, we are, as it were, in the era of Bleriot in relation to flying? We have barely started. We hardly have a clue about the interlocking complexities of the results of our actions, which are expanding and accelerating as time passes.

Neither do we have a clue about the timescales involved in the results of our actions. Certainly there are theories based on our present level of understanding. These theories change regularly. The effects of the changes we are causing now will certainly last for decades, probably for thousands and very possibly for millions of years.

Nor do we know what unforeseen future changes we may be triggering in the medium or long term: we are guessing. We do not know the outcome of the game we are playing with our earth.

In the meantime, in the face of this relative ignorance, the over-riding mantra is, even in the richest and most significant countries, 'our economy must not suffer and certainly not my pocket'. The important consideration is the here and now, and my standard of living, and certainly not the future of our descendants or of our planet.

Through global warming we may be changing our atmosphere, our climate, our seas and our land, and much of what lives in the seas and on the land. Maybe almost everything. We do not know for certain, but it seems feasible. Species are already becoming extinct thanks to our activities.

So Mankind, or some of it, is talking about what to do. 'Reduce the rate of increase in this warming' is Mankind's answer to the worldwide situation. But remember, without affecting my, or my nation's, standard of living.

It is intriguing to consider that going wholeheartedly for *cessation* of global warming would almost certainly provide a huge boost to the whole world's economy and greatly reduce the cost of living in developed countries. While some countries are feebly considering how much (or little) of their energy needs should be met by renewable sources, other countries are manufacturing and selling solar panels, wind turbines and so on – developing technologies and industries of the future. It is suggested that less than 2 per cent of Britain's power is produced by renewables compared with over forty per cent of Sweden's, with Norway producing even more. Expertise in building homes with minimal energy needs is another developing industry. As is designing equipment with greatly reduced energy needs.

Our house should generate about 1.5 megawatt hours of electricity a year; others with better-placed photovoltaic solar panels will certainly generate more, up to 2 megawatt hours a year for a standard domestic array (which would be about half our personal annual electricity usage). I estimate that 4380 such houses should be enough to generate the equivalent of 1 MWh continuously throughout the year.

If houses and appliances were designed for minimal power use, then even 1.5 megawatt hours a year would be a large percentage of a household's power needs – and if you are generating your own electricity you are not paying for it, while your country is not importing the fuel to produce it. Already in Britain you actually benefit financially from the electricity you generate, one way or another; how much depending on which electricity company you are with. In other countries you have been able to get an even better deal for years. Now, in this country, a newly installed household photovoltaic panel array could earn well over £800 a year financially, while also providing electricity to the household worth around £120. These figures must be approximate, referring to a normal household array on a south-facing roof with a clear view of the sky and should hold good for 25 years, with annual increments in line with inflation.

Do you get your money back on your investment? With photovoltaic panels, not for a number of years. We also have water-heating panels which provide us with our hot water from April to September so water-heating panels probably pay for themselves more quickly. And how quickly do you get your money back when you buy a car, which may well cost as much as an entire solar panel system, or much more?

But that is not the point, anyway. When we bought our first reduced wattage light bulb it cost £14. Now they are available for around £1.30 or less. Should we have waited? Certainly not!

There are two reasons why not. First, if everyone said, 'I'll wait till the price comes down: let other suckers pay the original high price,' then no one would buy any and the bulbs would cease to be available.

Second, each 100-watt equivalent bulb is supposed to save £7 a year on electricity costs if it is used regularly. Certainly, when we fitted a number of them our electricity use fell noticeably, and thus our bill. So, if everyone had refused to buy them when they were expensive then *everyone would have been a financial loser for years to come.* Everyone.

Many forms of renewable energy production are in their infancy and will presumably become much more efficient and cheaper over time. As with the light bulb, this would be a very poor reason for not investing in them now. To encourage and develop the manufacture and use of them in future years, there must be a market for them NOW. And they will continue to reduce living costs for years, especially if the cost of energy rises year by year.

And yet in many areas of the world, while there is much talk of 'green' policies, these are 'niche' concerns when you get down to it. In many democracies you are not going to gather many votes by proposing that individual voters should pay anything towards treating our planet better – even if each of them would benefit in the long term. For many voters the planet's problems do not even exist. And why on earth should dictatorships or other authoritarian systems of government concern themselves with the planet's future? Keeping themselves in power today is far more important.

Just how vigorously is the developed world leading us all towards a truly sustainable future? Are we fiddling a comforting tune while the planet heats up?

One might have supposed that, if an advanced species could know about the state of its planet, it would automatically always be monitoring what it could be doing to keep the planet stable and healthy, whatever might be the cause of any threat.

Indeed, would it be ridiculous to suggest that the state of the planet could be *expected* to be one of the prime considerations of any advanced species? For governments, might you expect it to be even more important than developing more powerful weapons, maintaining huge armies or waging wars? For individuals, even more important than amassing energy-requiring possessions?

An extension to this suggestion might be consideration of possible or probable future threats. We might even, as an advanced species, concern ourselves seriously with what might be going to happen, such as a large meteor strike, something that we know has happened before. As seriously as we concern ourselves with 'wars on terror', even.

Yellowstone Park may be a gigantic volcano waiting to explode as it did thousands of years ago. Indeed, such an explosion may be overdue. What is Mankind's contingency plan for such an event, which, it is suggested, might cause all crops to fail worldwide for three or more years?

Or is it plain silly to have any plan at all for a possible future catastrophic event? Is the future simply *their* problem and nothing whatsoever to do with *us*? Even if it may happen tomorrow?

Our first responsibility to our planet is how we manage our daily lives. Through the management of our daily lives we are steadily degrading our planet as our way of fulfilling this first responsibility, and at an ever-increasing rate worldwide.

Disinformation

Can it be that we are entering a disinformation era?

I do realise that there have been spectacular hoaxes over the centuries, achieving amazing success, and that it has never been wise to accept all 'facts' as actual facts.

However, we now have worldwide 24-hour news and information coverage in a vast range of media. There is absolutely no way that such a plethora of news sources can produce consistently reliable news or information. So we are being flooded with 'facts' without any simple way of checking their accuracy.

Two intriguing examples follow.

A man lost the end of his finger and, thanks to some miracle medication, was enabled to regrow the lost part. This major medical breakthrough was publicised around the world in various media over a number of years, with before and after photographs which clearly showed that this medication was spectacularly successful. This was clearly a real event and the photographs appeared to be (and were) genuine.

Some years ago I carelessly chopped off the end of my thumb with a machete. Today you cannot tell which thumb it was. The magical medical intervention that I received was a dressing and sticking plaster, renewed over several weeks.

In fact, as the doctor said as soon as he saw my thumb, the

ends of human digits can regrow, provided not too much has been chopped off. And behold, a doctor who saw the published photograph of the other man's finger pointed out that the photo clearly showed that the finger would regrow, by itself.

So, a real event, repeatedly published around the world over years thanks to modern media – and it was complete nonsense. Absolutely no medical breakthrough whatsoever.

The other example was a most unpleasant crowd confrontation in Northern Ireland. This was shown on television and one could see that this was a very dangerous situation – until the camera tracked back and you realised that about ten men were confronting rather more policemen on a path in a field. If the camera had not tracked back, one was apparently seeing clear evidence of the fragile nature of society in Northern Ireland. And just how often do we know that we are seeing, literally, the whole picture? You might also ask, why were ten angry men in a field being shown to the world at all?

Surely this mass acceptance of disinformation applies right across the spectrum of knowledge today? A newspaper article comparing wind and nuclear power explains that a nuclear power station has a life of 50 years (not rather longer?) while windpower has a life of 15 years.

Presumably this 15 years does mean something. But is it that the tower supporting the turbine only lasts 15 years? Really? Why is the Eiffel Tower still standing? Is it that the turbine only lasts 15 years? And cannot be replaced? Is it that the blades only last 15 years? And cannot be replaced?

Then, presumably on the basis of this 'information', the cost of wind-generated and nuclear-generated electricity is given: 5.42p a unit for wind and 2.8p a unit for nuclear. Really?

It is not just that the magical 15-year figure seems incomprehensible. What if the foundations and tower lasted 100 years with the turbine and blades being replaced at intervals? Is such a situation impossible? Would this affect the 5.42p figure?

Are we also to accept without question that the 2.8p a unit cost for nuclear really includes the cost of building the power station, running it, decommissioning it and storing the radioactive waste for some 50,000 years? Are our present storage systems for radioactive waste splendidly efficient and foolproof? Is it clearly established where and how the power stations' radioactive waste will be stored for thousands of years? What is the cost of storage based on?

Of course, it may be that the 15 years and the 2.8p figures are meaningful, soundly based and totally accurate. Not disinformation at all. One wonders, though, considering the overall accuracy of news stories. One could also wonder why such figures are published without any explanation as to how they were arrived at.

The problem also comes much nearer to home, though. I have mentioned our solar panels, photo-voltaic and water heating which produce about a third of our electricity and all our summer hot water and are therefore definitely green. When we were considering them, I did ask how much energy was involved in making them in the first place, but this information was not available. We guess that, over their working lifetime, they will more than replace the energy involved in their creation. If not, they are not green at all. We have to guess, because such information is not, in the twenty-first century, readily available.

What is readily available is such vital daily (hourly?) information as the number of knife crimes, murders and suchlike, so that we all know that we now live in a 'broken society', that it is not safe to walk the streets and that life today is far less satisfactory 'than it used to be'. When? In Victorian times, when people used to live by 'Victorian Values'? In the 1950s – 'no dogs, no coloureds'? In the days of the Mods, Rockers and biking gangs? In the days of football hooliganism?

A whole nation's attitude to itself can nowadays, in our enlightened times, be moulded by continuous outpourings of partial facts. Maybe disinformation sells, while impartial, dispassionate argument does not.

Some random twenty-first century questions

- Which methods of power production are the most cost-effective and the least harmful, not in the short term but over time?
- Do low wattage bulbs require more energy to produce than incandescent ones? If so, how much more? Are they safe to throw away?
- Does the earth's human population size matter to us or to our descendants?
- Is our country (or yours) building houses, offices and factories 'fit for our planet'? In other words, do our buildings function in harmony with our planet, or make demands upon it?
- If some countries are far more violent than others, is this of any significance? Or, if some countries are far less violent than others, is there anything to be learned from this?
- Do any countries produce an annual audit, on an internationally agreed basis, laying out their credentials? Education levels, crime statistics, energy production including methods, energy usage, food production, minimum wage, housing availability and cost, health care availability and cost, and so on. Or a five-year audit? Or any audit at all?

These questions are of various kinds: do they, or any of them, actually have answers? If they do, should the world's population have ready access to the answers? If not, why not? Is readily available accurate information really impossible to provide?

Throughout the twenty-first century shall we, on the one hand, continue to swallow disinformation avidly? And, on the other hand, never realise that real information, that we should want to know, just does not reach us?

With 24-hours news and multiple media competing, is Mankind entering a disinformation era?

Genetic Engineering

The new knowledge being ushered in by our present rudimentary understanding of our genome and those of other creatures and plants has huge potential for good or ill. Surely the crucial word here is 'rudimentary'?

Surely we know about as much about the genome now as doctors knew about disease in the eighteenth century? Would you rush to put one of those doctors in charge of your nation's Health Service today?

Surely it behoves us to move very very slowly and cautiously in developing the use of this new technology. Our past rush to use new technologies has invariably left subsequent generations to deal with 'unforeseen' problems. Or with problems that could perfectly well have been foreseen – or that were even explained before the technology was used, as with indiscriminate use of antibiotics.

Our track record should surely be a very sobering influence, when we come to make use of such a fundamental new discovery, fundamental to life itself?

How should we regard such fundamental new knowledge? As a species either you embrace the idea that always searching for further knowledge is a positive and desirable trait, or you decide that pursuing some knowledge may lead to outcomes that are too dangerous to acquire.

Can the human species really go for 'selected knowledge', deciding to shut down areas of research altogether?

Evolution has brought us to a position where we can and do circumvent evolution, in some respects. Some of those individuals who would have been eliminated through normal evolutionary pressures are now rightly valued. However, at the moment we are in a strange position. On the one hand we have the ability slightly to modify our own evolution; on the other hand we are just beginning to learn how we could radically fashion our own evolution through genetic sciences. This seems to be a threshold of potentially unlimited possibilities – and unlimited dangers.

On the one hand, when DNA first emerged on earth, it would have been perfectly reasonable to assume that, given time, some creatures on the planet would discover the building blocks of life and learn how to manipulate them. So what we are learning now was predictable and is perfectly reasonable.

On the other hand, when life first began on earth, it might also have been perfectly reasonable to suppose that these creatures, by the time they had discovered genes and how to manipulate them, would also have matured into a responsible and positive species, routinely acting in the general interest and always mindful of the short-, medium- and long-term consequences of their actions. A reasonable assumption, maybe, but clearly utterly misguided.

On all past performance indicators Mankind will rush headlong into genetic manipulation with some beneficial results, especially in medicine, some harmful and some potentially or actually catastrophic.

If you build tower blocks which turn out to be unsatisfactory living spaces, you can blow them up 30 years later. If you contaminate land with chemical or radioactive pollutants you can probably clear up the dangerous mess if you are prepared to spend millions. If new technology enables you to destroy, very swiftly, habitats and ecosystems which turn out to be crucial, you may, if you are lucky, be able to restore them, again probably at huge cost. If you completely fish out an area of the sea, rendering it largely sterile so that the entire fisheries industry is wiped out, the area might become restocked naturally, given maybe several hundred years.

By cross-breeding naturally occurring species using naturally occurring qualities within the species Mankind has developed a whole range of products with much enhanced features, though some are quite grotesque and perhaps a few actually dangerous, such as the alleged 'killer bees'.

The double helix was understood only some 50 years ago. Our own genome is still being deciphered. Not long ago we were told that vast stretches of our genome appear to have no function, which would seem to be most remarkable. This is surely a science in its absolute infancy.

However, various solutions to world food problems are already being offered by very large companies, solutions created by laboratory manipulation of genes, the results of which are allegedly completely understood.

Surely it is entirely reasonable to suspect that releasing artificially created genes into the environment, when the whole science is only some 50 years old, is like diving off a cliff in the dark, hoping that there is water below? Surely, once a newly created gene is out there in the environment there is no way whatsoever of recalling it if it turns out to have ghastly unforeseen consequences?

Do science and technology have a history of always being

right; of always predicting outcomes accurately? Does the world food shortage actually exist, and if it does, could it be addressed by far simpler and better-understood methods and strategies?

Then there is our nascent ability to modify humans themselves. Should we stop all use of genetic manipulation of our offspring, allow such use freely or make rules about what is and is not allowed in the way of such manipulation?

To try to stop all use would be an option, but would surely never work world-wide. It is true that the use of chemical warfare has so far been very greatly restricted world-wide, but this is a solely damaging invention, which may well rebound upon the user to great disadvantage. So far nuclear weapons have only been used twice, but they also may have great disadvantages for the user. But to stop all use world-wide of a new technique that has benign potential seems a complete non-starter.

However, there are all kinds of reasons for caution in this field. First and foremost is the timing. Is Mankind ready to use such a powerful discipline positively? Surely the most likely use of widespread genetic manipulation, considering Mankind's present mindset, is to make a profit?

Secondly, Mankind always considers short-term outcomes. The outcomes of much genetic manipulation are likely to be open-ended – not even just long term. Releasing DDT into the environment has had very long-term, originally unforeseen, outcomes but one may hope they can be eradicated, eventually. Can the long-term ramifications of releasing genetically modified life, plant or otherwise, into the environment be more confidently predicted than releasing chemicals or introducing foreign species, both of which have been done with extremely unfortunate results? The fact that, in most cases, resident species have proved resilient and survived new introductions does not alter the fact that some introductions have been very negative indeed.

48

Thirdly, the double helix was only recently understood. Is it credible that a 50-year-old science already has the keys to 'saving Mankind', and that its possible negative outcomes are genuinely understood?

Genuine medical use of genetic modification is already having splendid results, presumably with the ethical issues normally well considered. We must hope that any possible open-ended effects are clearly understood and evaluated.

However, cosmetic and 'improving' use of human genetic modification is an absolute can of worms, surely? You start with the notion that no child *need* be born with a defect (such as spina bifida). Seems reasonable.

If that becomes an established and accepted idea, the next step is that no child *should* be born with such a defect – or deafness, or asthma and so on. Or born a girl in some parts of the world. Clearly this is a potential disaster area.

And finally you arrive at the idea that every human child should be born as near 'perfect' as possible. A complete disaster for Mankind, whose ability to make such decisions is clearly absolutely nil. How ready are we for this new threshold?

Cooperation

Evolution is based on competition between species to ensure that the successful ones flourish. Thus competition appears to be crucial for the successful development and progress of life on earth (and maybe throughout the universe).

However, surely much may hinge on the word 'between' in the first paragraph?

Within some species, cooperation has been developed to an extraordinary degree, and species such as ants and bees were around and flourishing long before we emerged.

Within an ants' nest or a beehive it would not make a lot of sense for the workers to compete among each other to prove which is the best worker or soldier. The success of the hive depends on the success of each individual. It may be that in a hive workers that return drunk are dealt with drastically, but I do not imagine that any bee or ant is trying to undermine any other to gain competitive advantage. Neither a bee nor an ant would see much sense in that, I would have thought, except in the case of a queen killing other queen grubs before they can emerge. This drastic action is built into the survival of the whole nest and is for the common good.

Creatures that live in herds, flocks or shoals appear to be

living as a cooperating group rather than regularly competing with each other.

Even if mutual acceptance, never mind actual cooperation were not widespread throughout other species, Mankind is allegedly a step up from the rest of life on earth, by virtue of greatly enhanced 'intelligence'. A disinterested observer might imagine that greater intelligence would lead to a much greater degree of cooperation coupled with an even lower level of aggression and conflict than might be found in lesser species.

Certainly human individuals and groups cooperate and also come to each other's aid when there is need. There are many charities around the world doing wonderful work all the time. But still, so far at least, wholesale cooperation has hardly been a *distinguishing* feature of Mankind, regarded as a species rather than individuals, especially when compared with all the rest of the world's life-forms. The history of Mankind is not exclusively about wars and conflict, but one could hardly maintain that they are an insignificant part of Mankind's history.

Indeed, might one perhaps expect that, in the most advanced species on the planet, cooperation might hugely predominate over competition? Almost exclusively? Purely for practical and evolutionary reasons?

Charitable work is now rightly valued and praised: it addresses many problems, such as those caused by inadequate housing in the richest countries in the world, the awful results of torture and wrongful imprisonment, the fact that huge numbers of people in the world do not have ready access to clean, safe water, the problems caused by the immense disparity between the rich and the poor across the world, by incompetent or corrupt governments and of course by the dreadful results of war and conflict.

All the charities involved in these areas are highly commendable – but why do they exist? For example, the Red Cross/ Crescent was born out of the indecisive battle of Solferino where Henri Dunant was appalled by the tens of thousands of dead and dying left on the battlefield.

If care for all others were fundamentally rooted in governance, local, regional and international, as our species' primary concern, would these charities exist? Indeed, would the functions they perform even be regarded as 'charitable' at all? Should the building of roads, schools and hospitals be regarded as 'virtuous' in the same sense as the activities of Shared Interest, Shelter, Amnesty or Water Aid? Or would the need for such charities simply not exist if Mankind's governance was rooted in the welfare of all?

Competition stems from our evolutionary past, we are told, while our 'intelligence' sets us apart from the rest of life. It seems that we have chosen to use our 'intelligence' to institutionalise and codify competition around the planet rather than universal cooperation.

Is it fanciful to suppose that, if other planets have advanced life-forms, some (most?) of them might have universal cooperation instead of competition within species, within groups and between individuals as a powerful evolutionary driving force?

On earth, within groups, there is often a pecking order as well as a deal of cooperation. A pecking order is presumably necessary for stability within many groups, in order that they may have coherence and leadership. This need for leadership also clearly applies to Mankind, but is surely quite separate from random competitiveness and conflict?

Is this notion of universal cooperation utopian nonsense? If so, why? Can it be that Mankind cannot financially afford to value every individual equally? Or does not want to? Or does not know how to, not being a truly intelligent species?

Or should we perhaps expect no more of human governance than largely a process of continuous damage limitation, always attempting to cope with the results of earlier mismanagement?

Surely not?

Failure

What is failure? Evolution is described as 'the survival of the fittest'. Presumably this implies the 'failure of the weaker'? So it would seem that failure is 'a fact of life'. But maybe it is not as simple as that.

Mankind has been around for some three million years and has made, done and achieved many things. A success story? If Mankind lasts another 197 million years or so we shall have lasted about as long as the dinosaurs. But then, of course, they have not survived. So do we describe them as a failure?

Anaerobic cells inhabited the earth some three billion years ago and inhabit parts of the earth now, including our stomachs. If Mankind lasts another 2,997,000,000 years or so, we shall have lasted about as long as our anaerobic precursors have lasted so far.

So the fact that we have managed to last three million years has nothing whatsoever to do with success or failure. It is like scoring one run on the first ball in a five-day cricket match and announcing, 'success!'

Surely 'survival of the fittest' can be regarded as only involving success? The whole rationale is that the system throws up new species or alters existing ones to make the most of the life possibilities offered by the planet. So whether a species lasts a billion years, a million, a hundred, one generation or one individual, it is an experiment in the great scheme of things.

So is it reasonable to say that there is no such thing as failure in the great adventure of evolution, only continuous experimentation?

Mankind has made, done and achieved many things in our three million years. Millions of the earth's original cells began to create massive quantities of oxygen as a mere by-product of using the sun's energy to live and grow. With time, plants evolved from these original cells and are also to this day creating oxygen as a by-product of living.

Almost all living creatures that have ever inhabited our earth, or probably ever will, have only been able to exist because of the oxygen thus created. Nothing, absolutely nothing, that Mankind has so far achieved rates anywhere remotely near the achievement of those minute precursors of ours. The only comparable achievement that seems open to us might be achieving a mass extinction of almost all life on earth, maybe including our own. (An impossibility?)

Do we achieve as much in the great web of life as worms, bacteria, or plants have been routinely achieving day and night for many millions of years?

However, we know what we are doing, whereas they have no awareness of their achievements.

And now we really do enter the realms of failure!

Mankind has claimed 'intelligence' as an over-riding distinguishing feature, uses the ability to solve problems as one measure of this ability – and then routinely fails to solve the problems that really matter most. Indeed, 'the ability to create problems' might well be a truer distinguishing feature of Mankind, so far.

Violence

Violence is failure. War is failure. Of course a few wars or military interventions rescue people from dreadful situations, but these situations should never occur in the first place. The fact that they have occurred means that the whole situation is one of failure.

Whether it is bullying at school, terrorism, war or any other form of violence, it represents failure. In the cases of bullying and terrorism, failure by those perpetrating them, and in the case of war, either by those instigating wars or by those who have produced a situation in which war occurs.

If violence is not failure, then 'it is a fact of life'. What violence?

A carnivore kills its prey in order to eat it and live. This is a fact of life. Indeed, in some situations it might be that, if the predator is removed, the prey might suffer, as the balance of survival could be skewed causing overpopulation and population decline.

However, surely action whose *aim* is to cause pain or distress should have no place whatsoever as a 'fact of life' in the life of any species describing itself as 'intelligent'? Indeed, how many species that we classify as *un*intelligent actually commit gratuitous violence within their own species? Surely an 'intelligent' species descends into failure every time it sinks to violence? Similarly any individual within the species.

Does not this apply even to self-defence? I am 76. It seems likely that some 50 million people died that I might reach this age. My mother was from a Jewish family and I might well not have reached my teens if our side had not won the 1939–45 world war. I am, of course, immensely grateful that I have reached this age, but can this situation of some 50 million people dying that I might live be described honestly as 'success'?

An individual who has to use violence in self-defence is in a situation that should never occur; surely one in which the attacker has ceased to be a properly functioning human being?

The use of violence involves failure on two levels. First, the action itself shows the individual or group is malfunctioning. Torturers will damage or destroy their victims, but surely they will be doing similar damage to themselves, rendering themselves less than human, whatever their special 'justification'. Second, the result of using violence to 'solve' problems will cause more problems. 'The Balkan problems', Palestine, 'the Irish Troubles' (in 1166 the King of Leinster most unwisely asked the Anglo-Normans to come to help him fight the High King, Rory O'Connor; once invited, the Anglo-Normans were in no hurry to leave) are all around 1000 years old or more. Initial violence causes repeated violence to echo down the centuries.

And yet, do we regard violence as failure? Or fun? It is said that enjoying watching violence in films, or using it in the virtual reality of computer games, is entirely different from using it in real life. As with watching bear-baiting? Presumably enjoying watching murder in the Coliseum was fun and also tells us nothing about the values of the time.

Is it, however, completely naïve to imagine that, for a *truly* intelligent species, enjoying watching violence could be incomprehensible? Or even seen as degrading for the viewer? Are there not now groups of humans for whom the use or enjoyment of violence is entirely foreign, and have there perhaps been others in the past?

Or is violence built into Mankind's make-up? A basic fault? If so, why are most humans not violent in their daily lives? Many of those who use violence grow to believe that it was wrong to have used it. Can Mankind do the same?

Other individuals remain violent all their lives. Herein lies a question. Are such individuals fully functioning members of the human species, or do they have a dangerous flaw, like a car with faulty brakes? If an individual cannot be allowed to live freely in the society of other humans, because (s)he will harm other humans, can that individual be a fully functioning human, in the sense that all the others are?

Is a violent person ill? Can a violent person be cured? If not now, is it an impossible notion that in 500 or 1000 years our descendants may understand the problem in a way we cannot, and be capable of curing people 'suffering from violence'? Our ancestors used to 'know' that it was the Humours that made us ill, but now we have different ideas.

Mankind suffers from violence. Is Mankind ill? If so, can Mankind cure itself?

Population

We, unlike all other creatures, can count our numbers and now to some extent can quantify the effect we have on our environment. Being able to do this, we have been choosing to populate our environment to such an extent that we are forced to alter it dramatically without, until recently, having any idea of, or interest in, the effect these alterations will have. As a species we could presumably have long since decided to fit ourselves into our available environment. Some groups have been exhorted, not to procreate thoughtfully, but to 'go forth and multiply' because, presumably, if there are twice as many humans in 2500 as in 2000 there will be twice as much goodness and happiness. Really?

If the 6,000,000,000 world population gradually reduced to 3,000,000,000 would there be so few people that they would not be able to produce enough food (for half the present number) or even cope with modern life at all?

As a specific example, there are some 60,000,000 people in the United Kingdom now. If this number were gradually reduced to half there would still be 30,000,000. Would this mean that life in Britain's cities, towns and countryside would be necessarily greatly impoverished for the 30,000,000? Would the requirements for half as much food, fuel, transport and general consumption be a serious disadvantage? The population of Norway, with a rather greater land mass than the UK, is around 5,000,000: are they all in dire straits?

However, levels of emigration and immigration are utterly irrelevant. It is the size of the whole world's population, Mankind's attitude towards its size and the demands that the population places upon the planet now and in the future that are the crucial considerations.

Would, perhaps, an intelligent species on a planet of earth's size decide that, as 400 individuals were too few to sustain a full life for all and 400 billion too many for the planet comfortably to sustain a full life for all, there would be a rough optimum target size for the species to aim at? Would any intelligent species be able to stabilise its population once it had decided to do so?

Or does intelligence demand that planetary population size should always be left to chance, war, disease and shortage of food, water and resources?

Is it a sign of intelligence for a species to 'master' its habitat in response to ever-increasing demands that it places on that habitat, rather than to live as a species in harmony with its environment? Is a city of 25 million inhabitants an achievement or a nonsense? Is the steady extinction of species, including our near relatives, apes and monkeys, to accommodate a few more millions of ourselves an achievement or stupidity?

Now 35,000 years is quite a long span of time in human history. It seems that the Aborigines in Australia lived successfully in that seemingly inhospitable environment for 35,000 years before the more 'advanced' white man arrived with rabbits and rats and the enlightened notion of using the continent as a prison. The Aborigines' success stemmed directly from their affinity with, and understanding of, the environment in which they lived. They shared the environment with the creatures and plants that lived in it.

Of course, the Aborigines only lived as hunter-gatherers, creating very little apart from a stable society lasting three and a half times as long as the time Britain has been inhabited since the last Ice Age, as well as oral literature and cave art.

Is a half-way house an impossibility? A situation in which Mankind lives in societies stable over thousands of years, developing thought, art and practical invention and creation, and yet all the while living in harmony with other societies and with its environment?

It seems that there were, and may still be, Indian tribes in Colombia, such as the Yucuba, living in the forest. They believed that their environment was 'on loan' to them and that they should pass it on to their descendants in as good condition as they found it. Another of their ways of thought was that, if one of them acquired too many possessions, he or she would begin to feel uncomfortable and so would give many of them away. Too many possessions *diminished* the individual's feeling of worth.

These two groups are, of course, only 'natives' without any true understanding of market economics, mass education, information technology, the universe, space flight or the Industrial Revolution.

Nonetheless, is it absolutely clear that it is really foolish and misguided to believe that each generation has our environment 'on trust' and that too many possessions diminish the individual? Would our visitor from space perhaps feel quite at home with such notions, if it/(s)he functioned by cooperation rather than by competition?

Or must we believe that any visitor from space would agree that the environment is there for our use today, irrespective of the effects of our use, and that the more possessions you acquire, the more you are a complete person?

The Middle Ages

We live now in the Middle Ages. At least, we must sincerely hope that we do. We must surely hope that in AD 3000 they will look back to, say, the period between the building of the first towns and, say, AD 2500 as a single period – the Middle Ages, when only individuals and small groups could see that the way Mankind as a whole was acting was seriously flawed.

We must hope that they will see this as a finite historical period when Mankind used to see the following as normal:

- Wars around the world – the Assyrians; the Babylonians; the Roman conquests; the Hundred Years War; Turkish/Moorish invasions of Europe, India, Egypt etc; routine wars throughout Europe through the centuries; Napoleon; the Franco-Prussian War; the First World War (some 20+ million died); the Second World War (some 40+ million died); Korea; Iraq and so on – and these combatants were the most advanced, most 'civilised' countries in the world, of their times.
- Ever more lethal weapons being devised continuously.
- Torture – latterly used worldwide by democracies as well as dictatorships, and refined by using technology.

- Widespread poverty and starvation.
- Some humans being immensely wealthy while others were extremely poor.
- Diseases which could have been eradicated being widespread.
- The earth's climate being radically changed without understanding many of the implications.
- The earth's ecology being radically changed without understanding many of the implications.
- Huge decisions being taken with little or no concern for their long-term consequences.
- No clean water for a large percentage of the world's population, while a small percentage had it on tap in their own homes.
- Indiscriminate use of the earth's resources, as if they would last for ever.
- Minimal acceptance that we had any real responsibility for our planet, or for the other species with which we share it.

and so on and on . . .

It is good to know that in the twenty-first century there are stirrings of concern for some of these issues. It would be even better to believe that genuine, meaningful and robust action is being taken worldwide to deal with them quickly and effectively. It would be good indeed if one could!

We must surely hope that our descendants will have advanced completely beyond these primitive and increasingly dangerous behaviours by the year 3000. Or maybe, by then, these Middle Ages of ours may seem a Golden Age, before the effects of Mankind's present actions had really affected the earth . . .

Global Warming

Mankind is faced with problems, many of them of our own creation: pollution, flooding, poverty, war and so on. Global warming is very likely to be one such problem, *irrespective of the cause*.

For some of Mankind, faced with this apparent problem, the argument is simple: 'Global warming is not happening, or if it is happening it is nothing to do with humans. But, if it is happening and it is caused by humans, nothing can be done about it anyway. If something can be done about it, it would be far too expensive and affect the economy adversely. And if something could be done about it without the economy collapsing, someone else should be doing it. It is no good if one country does something, so other countries should be leading the way. And anyway, why should I do anything? I cannot possibly do anything useful, and if I did it would affect my quality of life.'

Perhaps there is another, perverse (?) way of looking at this. Global warming appears to be happening and is probably caused or exacerbated by humans. Might it be sensible for every individual human to wish to help in stabilising the planet's climate at its present relatively benign state, whatever the cause of the changes?

Why 'whatever the cause'? If the climate is warming and carbon dioxide in the atmosphere is increasing steadily, why does it matter what is causing it? It is now suggested that the 280 parts per million ratio of carbon dioxide in the air before the Industrial Revolution has reached 386 ppm (an increase of 37%) and is increasing at around 2 ppm a year and so may be 400 ppm by 2016, an almost 42% increase. The effects are just the same whatever may be the cause, rising planet temperature and a change in the chemical composition of the seas being two of them.

Why 'every individual'? Because the six billion or so of us are not some imaginary total – Mankind is six billion individuals. If I say, 'Why should I do anything?', then all six billion have an equal right to say the same. If I do nothing no one should do anything.

Mankind (or some of it) has indeed announced that an attempt should be made to reduce somewhat the rate of growth in the production of pollutants causing the warming (or may be causing the possible warming, if you are a sceptic).

You might think that all of Mankind would agree. There is certainly much verbiage on the subject. Some countries have achieved 40% or more of non-polluting energy production, some 2%, some 1% and some 0%. And just because a country has only achieved 2% certainly does not stop that country from trumpeting its green credentials worldwide. Some would say that actions speak louder than hot air, especially on this subject.

Is Mankind genuinely committed to reducing global warming? Not reducing the rate of increase, but *actually reducing global warming*? Drastically? Reducing man-made greenhouse gases to nil?

Cannot

'Cannot' is an entirely successful concept. If it is agreed that something cannot be done, then this is a self-fulfilling prophecy.

I have been told by someone 'in the know' in the field of education administration that a child born profoundly deaf cannot learn to speak. I happen to know from long experience that this is *utter nonsense* – but, behold, if it is generally known that such a child cannot be taught to speak, then it becomes true. Why should anyone waste their time trying to do something that is known to be impossible?

Clearly it is impossible to produce all the world's energy needs from renewable sources. Why is it impossible? Because we know it cannot be done.

Of course there is some wind around, there are some tides and waves, there is a bit of geothermal energy available and vastly more of the sun's energy falls on a small part of most deserts in a day than Mankind could possibly use in a year. But can anyone seriously suggest that these unreliable sources could supply all our needs? Of course not – because we want it to be impossible.

Countries can maintain a standing army of a million soldiers to fight non-existent enemies, can initiate wars, can expend vast amounts of money, manpower and energy creating new weapons, manufacturing them and selling them around the world. But the idea of Mankind pooling this grotesque waste of money, labour and resources and using it instead for the good of the world and its future is presumably ridiculous – because it is impossible. It cannot be done. So it cannot.

Are all the materials and energy regarded as essential for the daily running of life in the developed countries (and soon to be equally essential in the developing countries) actually necessary and unavoidable? We are frequently told that technology is the way to give the world a secure and better future. This is like saying that a spade will dig the garden for you. If you do not have the will to dig, your spade will achieve nothing.

As well as using the wind, the waves and geothermal energy, would it be possible to use the virtually limitless amount of solar energy falling on our planet to create as much power as we all need? It seems that the sun is continuously breaking some seawater into oxygen and hydrogen – and hydrogen is an entirely non-polluting fuel. If the sun is doing it already, would it be impossible for Man to do it and on a grand scale, powering all our needs? Or to harness the magic of photosynthesis?

Would it be possible to build only carbon-neutral new houses?

Would it be possible to reduce, rather than increase, our power requirements, by 'needing' much less energy and by better or entirely novel designs?

It is said that Sweden already produces over 40% of its energy from renewable sources while Britain produces less than 2% so 'cannot' is a variable concept.

Was it possible to build harbours made of concrete in the 1940s, tow them across the Channel to Normandy and sink them to use as harbours for months to supply the invasion? Well, actually, yes, and they were called Mulberry Harbours.

Was it possible to sink a pipeline to the bottom of the Channel from England to France in 1944 so that petrol could be pumped to supply the armies of the invasion? Well, actually, yes, and it was called PLUTO.

Of course people could easily have said, 'You cannot do these things,' and if everyone had agreed, they would have been right.

This was done over half a century ago.

We are told that technology has come a long way since then

– but producing 100% of the world's energy needs by renewables? Impossible! Can't be done!

Solar panels

Virtually all life on earth depends on solar panels. Indeed, there might well be no life at all on the land without them. They were 'invented' about three billion years ago. We call them 'leaves' or, in the sea, 'algae' or 'seaweed'.

A leaf harnesses the sun's energy to use the materials in the air and the soil to create the plant – and animals eat the plants or other plant-eating animals. Insects eat the plants, their nectar or the animals that eat the plants. The plants regenerate the soil. So virtually all life on earth uses the sun's present energy to supply its needs – except Mankind.

Maybe we cannot expect Mankind to be as efficient as nature when it comes to invention, but if almost all life on the land only exists because nature invented solar panels, is it really impossible for Man to produce all our energy needs directly from the sun?

Is it impossible, then, for Mankind to do what grass does every day? Must Mankind really be the only species that plunders its planet, rather than lives in harmony with it? Must Mankind be the only species on earth (in the universe?) that does not live a renewable lifestyle?

Is it really inescapable that intelligence demands *using up* the planet's resources, rather than *using* them? Can intelligence never get 100% of the energy it claims to 'need' from the sun, which shines on the earth every second of every day, the winds, which are blowing every second of every day, the waves, which never cease, and the earth's own ever-present core heat?

Our Positive Features

If we share love, feeling, compassion, cooperation with our animal ancestors and present-day fellow creatures, are there areas in which Mankind has broken new ground, apart from the use of routine violence and wilful destruction?

Clearly abstract thought is one area which Mankind has developed far beyond the simple thought processes of our fellow creatures, but what of altogether new ground broken?

Could it be that 'useless behaviour' is our area of crowning achievement so far? Indeed, is it the one area of behaviour of which we can be genuinely proud to be human and different?

Art and music need not exist. They appear to be of no immediate practical use, apart from giving pleasure. They may well be therapeutic or socially reinforcing but these are by-products. Birds sing, but singing for them must surely be much involved with territory and mating strategies and thus largely practical, even if they may enjoy it as well. Bower birds decorate their chosen area – but to attract a mate.

But much of human art and music over the millennia has surely been created because the artist or composer felt compelled to do so? The products may give pleasure and earn money, but the driving force seems to come from within and not for a practical purpose.

73

If a highly advanced species visited earth with technology millennia in advance of ours, but without the least appreciation of art or music, how would humans rate this species? As superior – or as sadly deficient even if its members were fully cooperative and otherwise genuinely intelligent? Or could they not actually be intelligent if they could not appreciate abstract beauty?

Or could they, in their turn, maintain that, as all art is pointless, there is truly no point in 'appreciating' it?

Another area of apparently 'useless behaviour' is a sense of humour. Animals clearly have fun. As I write, a dog keeps encouraging a member of a family to come out onto the field with a tennis racket and hit a ball for the dog, tail wagging hugely, to fetch. The dog then returns near to the person, but will not give the ball back, so the person goes and sits down again. The dog then pauses a while, takes the ball to her and persuades her to do it all over again. The dog is organising the game and clearly enjoying it.

Telling and enjoying jokes is something else, different from just 'having fun'. Fun is enjoying doing something, which may be absurd, but humour concentrates on enjoying the absurd. The dog might have been enjoying the absurdity of refusing to give the ball back until the human had sat down, and other species may also occasionally enjoy similar situations, but for the human species a sense of humour, enjoyment of the absurd, is a very real and significant part of life.

Suppose this advanced species arrived on earth and was discovered by us to be utterly without a sense of humour. Once again, how would we rate them? As our superiors or as somehow deficient?

Surely all of our scientific, medical and practical achievements build upon the nascent abilities in animals. Surely, also, as DNA first begins to appear on any planet, an observer could say, 'Aha, they will probably venture into space one day,' with some confidence. But could the observer also say, 'Aha, they will create beautiful music and have a great sense of humour,' with equal confidence?

Are we the greatest because, while listening to our favourite CD and looking at the pictures on our wall, we know why the chicken crossed the road?

Thousand-year Thought

When any new course of action is proposed, by an individual or a government, how far ahead are the possible outcomes considered, and how thoroughly?

Five years seems normal in a democracy, where the outcome of the next election has to be borne in mind, although sometimes 20 or even 100 years are considered. On the other hand it sometimes seems as if absolutely no thought at all is given to the likely outcomes of decisions. Would one expect even as long a timespan in a dictatorship? To consider the possible outcomes of one's actions on a time-span reaching from tomorrow to a thousand years hence would, of course, be ridiculous! Why?

Deforestation can wreak changes which may last far more than a mere thousand years and may well be irreversible. Areas can lose all their topsoil and thus no longer be able to support significant plant life; downstream rivers can flood regularly on a huge scale, changing the landscape again for very long time periods.

A thousand years ago bows and arrows were the most powerful weapons and could kill thousands at a time. Now we can kill millions at a time. Is it illogical to imagine that, in a thousand years' time, our descendants will be able to kill billions at a time, if we carry on as we are?

Expanding unlimited consumer satisfaction exponentially across the planet, with known polluting results, is presumably going to change the climate in ways that we can only guess at, and very probably with effects lasting thousands of years.

Nuclear power stations are being built whose toxic waste will need safe storage by our descendants for maybe 50,000 or 100,000 years. Presumably those building them know now exactly how this storage will be accomplished for five or ten times the length of time since the last Ice Age. Also, presumably the sale of electricity for 60 or 70 years will cover not only the cost of building, running and decommissioning the power station but also funding 50,000 years of storage.

It might be that routine truly long-term thinking would restrict today's options – but might not the reverse be true? Might it rather stimulate thought and creativity? If today we build thousands of houses on flood plains and tomorrow sea levels rise and/or rainfall increases, will not the resultant problems have been avoidable? And would not today's option of rethinking the distribution of housing have been a creative and positive challenge?

As I write, the world is in a financial crisis. A total surprise appearing unexpectedly out of the blue . . . well hardly.

If today you are happy to live in a society built on huge amounts of personal debt combined with the selling worldwide of huge, barely understood financial packages, then when it goes wrong tomorrow, surprise seems a ridiculous response. But, some say, this is just 'the market adjusting itself'. Is this not like buying a car, knowing that the wheels will fall off every so often, but then intending to put them back on again, provided you survive the crash each time? The concept of forward planning does not seem to have been much of a priority here.

You may say that nothing designed by a human can be

expected to be perfect – but surely then the routine assessment of long-term outcomes would seem even more desirable? Even intelligent?

But you may say that trying to predict outcomes over a thousand-year period is both impossible and impractical. Another way of looking at this is to try to imagine what people in AD 3000 might think of the way we do things today, as we can now look back to AD 1000 and evaluate their activities.

Can we learn anything from making this comparison when arriving at decisions? Or are we really only capable of short-term thinking?

The lesser of two evils

Earlier I posed the question, 'Can a clever action which has an unfortunate and avoidable result ever be regarded as an intelligent action?' Presumably it could be if the result will be the lesser of two known evils. Is it tenable to suggest that Mankind's present behaviour represents the lesser of two evils?

If today we wish to pursue all our modern behaviours, should we regard the probable disastrous future results as a price that our descendants will consider worth paying?

Switching to entirely renewable energy for all our energy needs, focusing firmly on preserving the present ecology of our planet and ensuring that all of Mankind has a satisfying life, would be a huge undertaking and initially very expensive. Also a nuisance for those who are doing well under the present systems.

Accepting that violence, war, destruction and gross inequality are 'normal' for humans is far easier than deciding to reject them entirely.

So maybe the 'evil' of changing Mankind's present behaviour is greater than the evils we are visiting upon our fellow humans who are suffering the results now, and greater than the evils we shall be visiting upon our descendants. Would attempting to advance towards an intelligent future be a 'greater evil' than continuing as we are?

The Gods and the Universe

It seems logical that the gods of the twenty-first century should be the standard-bearers of Mankind's forward march towards a world in which Mankind lives in harmony as a species and in harmony with the planet we inhabit.

To start considering this proposition by claiming that God does not exist seems about as sensible as one amoeba assuring another amoeba that Mankind does not exist. The amoeba is presumably as capable of knowing the truth about Mankind as Mankind is of comprehending an omnipotent God, if God exists.

However, it might also seem reasonable to assume that any god is going to have at least as high standards of behaviour as one would expect from a decent citizen of the twenty-first century. Indeed, would it be fair to expect that our gods should have higher standards than humans?

- If any god insisted that the earth was the physical centre of the universe . . .
- If any god was involved in the burning alive of heretics . . .
- If any god was involved in slavery . . .
- If any god condoned initiating war between or within any religions . . .

- If any god did not value men and women equally and did not demand equal rights and responsibilities for each half of his human creation . . .
- If any god was homophobic . . .
- If any god proclaimed that humans should murder other humans if they transgress the god's regulations . . .
- If any god announced that any human not becoming a member of his organisation would go to hell . . .

then how should a decent citizen rate such a god?

'There is only one true God and He is not yours.' Is this a path that can be expected to lead all members of an advanced species to live together in harmony?

The gods of the twenty-first century maintain a number of extremely varied and sometimes conflicting notions. One apparently essential notion for several gods is that half of the world's population, women, are ineligible for most offices and positions in these gods' worship organisations – which many humans would call sex discrimination.

If a person announced officially that women were not suitable for posts within a company or an organisation, because they were women, this would nowadays hardly be greeted with approval in many parts of the world, surely? Especially, perhaps, as God, or evolution, has created approximately half of all humans women.

Acceptance of homosexual people, clergy and civil partnerships are other areas where the gods are divided. I believe that, in Britain earlier in my lifetime, homosexuality between consenting adults was a matter for the police while, at the same time, domestic violence was not.

Thank goodness, human goodness, we have moved beyond these disgraceful attitudes, just as we have moved beyond trial by ordeal, debtors' prisons, transportation for theft and other travesties of justice which were once widely accepted, at times when religion was a far more potent force than it is now. You might have thought that the gods of those days would have made certain such disgraceful acts would be rapidly brought to an end. However, as the gods used to sanction the burning alive of heretics, for example, that was not likely to happen.

If my neighbour is homophobic, sexist or violent I should regard his or her state of mind as an unfortunate weakness of character. Should I expect the gods of the twenty-first century to have higher standards than my neighbour – or is that asking too much of them? Or do the gods wish my neighbour to have lower standards?

Surely the notion of a homophobic, sexist or violent god is an oxymoron – just as the notion of a seven-foot-tall dwarf? You are either seven foot tall OR you may be a dwarf, but you certainly cannot be both. Surely you are either a god OR you are homophobic, sexist or violent.

At least one of the gods of the twentieth century was still most certainly racist, but maybe all of today's gods have given up on this.

Although some gods in the twenty-first century apparently favour the chopping off of limbs and the stoning of adulterers (normally female), other gods have, as already mentioned, abandoned the practice of burning witches and heretics alive, and now accept that the earth is not the physical centre of the universe.

So the gods change their minds – thank goodness! Can it indeed be that basic human goodness is what changes the gods' minds? Or even that basic human goodness is where the gods reside?

A few of the gods of the twenty-first century are indeed

already inclusive and positive: not differentiating in any way on the basis of sex, gender, sexual orientation and so on. Is it too much to hope that, one day, all of the earth's gods will be genuinely inclusive, as genuinely inclusive as we expect of a decent human being now? And that they will then all be in the forefront of helping to transform Mankind into a united species, at one with itself and with its whole environment?

Surely, too, omnipotence is a real problem? If humans, far from omnipotent, could in the far future populate fertile planets with beings whom they had genetically equipped to thrive in the different conditions on each particular planet, would we expect them deliberately to equip them with violence and short-term thinking among their various attributes? If so, why? Why would it be better to design such beings with these features?

Surely it would be nonsense to suggest that beings without these features would be too bland or uninteresting to be worth existence? Would they not still be prone to error, to failure, to disagreement – and still capable of great enlightenment, achievement, creativity? Surely it is ridiculous to suggest that an intelligent species is valueless unless it has violent and destructive qualities? Would anyone suggest that every parent should hope that their children and grandchildren will grow up violent and destructive?

And yet today's omnipotent gods are alleged to have done just that – to have created a 'top species' which is, uniquely, violent and destructive.

Can it be true that, if our far descendants fashion beings to inhabit other planets, they would be naive to exclude violence, destructiveness and short-sightedness from these beings – as these behaviours 'add to the texture of life'?

We have previously considered the 'Big Bang'. It may be that a god created our universe, or enabled it to occur. A universe which had at its very creation the potential to create life within it. The universe seems to create the requisite building blocks and to have a built-in 'requirement' for life to spring into being wherever and whenever it is remotely possible, at least to judge from our planet.

Surely such a creation, whether of our own universe (or perhaps countless numbers of universes) would be truly awesome, way beyond our ability to comprehend or appreciate, whether it just appeared or was created?

However, if it was created that would lead us back to the original question. Would this creator have so organised the building blocks, or the mechanisms involved in the emergence of life forms, that the most advanced species would, *in every case*, prove to be the only one on each planet to be routinely randomly violent and destructive?

Or would such a 'building-block creation' mean that every advanced species in the universe would have the capability to be entirely non-violent and non-destructive? Is such a thing possible, even theoretically?

If we posit an omnipotent creator, could such a being achieve such a universe? And if not, why not? It might be that such a creation would be beyond the powers of *any* god, but why?

Or are violence and destructiveness intrinsic to competitiveness and self-assertion, which are, in turn, essential to evolution? If the race for sperm to reach the ovum was not survival of the fittest, then less effective genes would be as likely to be propagated as the most effective. Then species would presumably not evolve successfully and the whole evolutionary process would fail.

So are violence and destructiveness as distinguishing features in the most advanced species a pay-off, to enable that species to reach that pinnacle in the first place?

Does evolution actually equate survival of the fittest with violence and destructiveness? There is clearly rivalry between individuals (usually males) in many species in mate selection, to ensure that the fittest genes are favoured. But even between rival males, fights to the death seem to be rare. Dangerous and pointless. If the dominant males were regularly seriously wounded in brutal combats, this would hardly be helpful in evolutionary terms.

In the animal world, violence between individuals in groups or between groups within a species is surely also rare? Again, dangerous and pointless for the individual and for the group. There may well be a 'pecking order' within the group, as part of the coherence and organisation of the group, and this order may be physically challenged as time passes, but if it were not so the whole group could suffer. Not violence for its own sake, at least as far as the whole group's welfare is concerned, but to safeguard the group's future.

There are species of monkeys that are routinely belligerent, one group with another and as individuals. However, it seems that the bonobo monkeys, which humans will probably soon extinguish, do not indulge in violence at all as individuals or as groups.

So where, in evolutionary terms, is the sense in the most advanced group on the planet being routinely violent and destructive? Would it really have been impossible for humans to have developed from bonobo? Did the monkeys that led to us and to the chimpanzees, another violent species apparently, really need to diverge in this manner from the rest of the earth's life forms, in order to make the final step? If so, why?

Why should achieving intelligence involve such a step? Such an apparently disadvantageous step? If these negative attributes were essential for the development of advanced species, then surely there could *never* be *any* truly intelligent species in the entire universe? A dismal prospect! And unlikely?

Whether the universe just happened or there was a creator, why should it be impossible for any, or indeed all, of the most advanced species to be, or to become over time, entirely cooperative and non-destructive?

Realpolitik

Realpolitik is supposed to mean organising society by 'facing reality' and only attempting the possible. Ostriches are supposed to put their heads in the sand to avoid facing reality . . .

Surely, to accept that the way things are traditionally run worldwide is the best way, is not facing reality at all? The status quo across the world is a dismal picture – and the status quo is what we have arrived at through the process of Realpolitik through thousands of years.

Let us raise our heads from the sand and consider the possibility of 'Unrealpolitik'.

The status quo on our planet

- Competition between states, blocks and groups is normal.
- Competition between individuals is frequent.
- The use of violence 'to achieve results' is endemic between nations, groups and some individuals.
- The planet is to be 'mastered' to fit the demands of the present day.
- The extinction of other species by our actions may be

unfortunate but is a small price worth paying for our advancement.

- Whatever problems we cause now can be rectified by technology in the hands of our descendants.
- What matters is the here and now. Assessing future outcomes of today's actions is a fool's game.
- The 'criminal classes' must be dealt with severely. In other words, criminality is a sin, and not a social malaise.
- The planet can accommodate a world population of any size whatever.
- Food, fuel and materials should always be as cheap to buy as possible. How they are produced is an irrelevance.
- Food, fuel and materials will never run short.

But what about philanthropy and the green revolution?

Mankind has indeed eradicated smallpox and some countries are beginning to have a green attitude to our planet. There are real moves to eradicate polio and drastically reduce or eliminate bilharzia.

Individuals, charities and even governments around the world are undertaking worthy causes every day. Fair Trade is a spreading phenomenon. All of this is highly commendable, of course. And that is the nub of the problem. None of this should be 'highly commendable'. There should be no Fair Trade.

There should only be fair trade. The only possible reason for introducing Fair Trade must be that trade is often not fair. Surely, if trade always gave a fair return for work done, then everyone around the world involved in trade, workers as well as bosses, would be able to use some of their earnings to buy from world trade, thus increasing world trade, while themselves achieving a satisfactory life?

Why should philanthropic actions be regarded as highly commendable? Because they are special and not the norm. Going to work each day is not regarded as 'highly commendable' – it is simply what one does.

As explained in the Foreword to this book, these thoughts are about Mankind as a species and not about individuals or their behaviour.

Is it impossible for Mankind to be, as a species, philanthropic – 'loving all humans'? And not merely for altruistic reasons, but because such a way of life would benefit every single individual on earth? Philanthropic out of practical self-interest. Philanthropic because it makes sense.

What If?

- Suppose an advanced species inhabiting a planet based its entire way of life on mutual cooperation for mutual benefit.
- Suppose the individuals within the species did the same.
- Suppose the concept of achieving any results at all through violence was completely unknown.
- Suppose all on the planet believed that they should hand their planet on to their descendants in as good condition as they found it when they were born.
- Suppose that *each* individual believed that *every* individual should have a comfortable sufficiency for a happy life.
- Suppose all believed that their actions and the outcomes of their actions should, to the best of their knowledge, harm no one and no creature or part of their planet, now or in the future.
- Suppose it was understood that any individual or group would always expect to assess the short-, medium- and long-term results of any action before undertaking it.
- Suppose every member of the species believed that, if any other member deliberately harmed anyone, both the perpetrator and the sufferer would need immediate help. The latter help to recover and the former help to return to a properly functioning state of mind.

93

- Suppose it was generally recognised that population size should be maintained well within the bounds of available resources.
- Suppose that, as a matter of course, readily renewable sources of food, fuel and materials were routinely used, including recycling wherever practicable, with non-renewable sources used sparingly if needed and avoided if alternatives could be developed, as a matter of principle.

Would this be a description of an intelligent species?

In a Nutshell

Can we regard the way we treat ourselves, our planet and all its inhabitants as intelligent, even by our own definition of intelligence?

If we are not yet '*Homo sapiens*' should we hope that we are '*Homo sapiens incipiens*'?

Have we, as a species, the ability to learn to act truly intelligently – *ultelligently*?

Shall we ever have the will to do so?

When might that be?

Too late?